Published by Creative Education
P.O. Box 227, Mankato, Minnesota 56002
Creative Education is an imprint of
The Creative Company
www.thecreativecompany.us

Design and production by The Design Lab
Art direction by Rita Marshall
Printed by Corporate Graphics
in the United States of America

Photographs by 123RF (Keith Levit), Alamy
(Danita Delimont), Corbis (Tim Davis, Steven
Kazlowski/Science Faction, Hans Strand, Kennan
Ward), Getty Images (Wayne R. Bilenduke, Darrell
Gulin, Pal Hermansen, Ralph Lee Hopkins, Norbert
Rosing), iStockphoto (Dean Fetterolf)

Library of Congress Cataloging-in-Publication Data
Bodden, Valerie.
Polar bears / by Valerie Bodden.
p. cm. — (Amazing animals)
Includes bibliographical references and index.
Summary: A basic exploration of the appearance,
behavior, and habitat of polar bears, Earth's biggest
land predators. Also included is a story from folklore
explaining why polar bears have short tails.
ISBN 978-1-58341-811-6
1. Polar bear—Juvenile literature. I. Title. II. Series.
QL737.C27B63 2010
599.786—dc22   2009002714

CPSIA: 092611 PO1507
9 8 7 6 5

AMAZING ANIMALS

POLAR BEARS

BY VALERIE BODDEN

CREATIVE EDUCATION

A polar bear's white color blends in with snow

Polar bears are big bears. They are the biggest land **predators** in the world! Polar bears live where there is lots of snow and ice.

predators animals that kill and eat other animals

Polar bears have thick fur. The fur is all white. The only part of a polar bear's body that does not have fur is its black nose. Polar bears have lots of fat under their skin to keep them warm.

Polar bears stay warm and cozy in freezing cold

Polar bears are huge animals. A male polar bear can weigh more than 1,500 pounds (680 kg). That is more than eight grown-up men put together! A polar bear standing on its back legs could touch the rim of a basketball hoop.

Polar bears sometimes stand up for a look around

Polar bears like areas with a lot of ice and water

Polar bears live in the **Arctic**. Most of the year, polar bears live on top of ice that covers the **ocean**. Some polar bears live on land for part of the year, too.

Arctic an area at the top of Earth where no trees grow

ocean a big area of deep, salty water

Polar bears eat meat. Their favorite food is seals. Sometimes polar bears eat whales or walruses, too.

Polar bears get most of their food from the ocean

Polar bear cubs come out of their den in the spring

Mother polar bears dig a **den** in deep snow. Soon, two **cubs** are born in the den. After a while, the cubs come out of the den. Their mother teaches them to hunt. Polar bears that are good hunters can live more than 20 years.

den a home that is hidden, like a cave

cubs baby bears

Grown polar bears spend their time alone. They do a lot of swimming. Polar bears can swim fast and far.

Big front paws make polar bears good swimmers

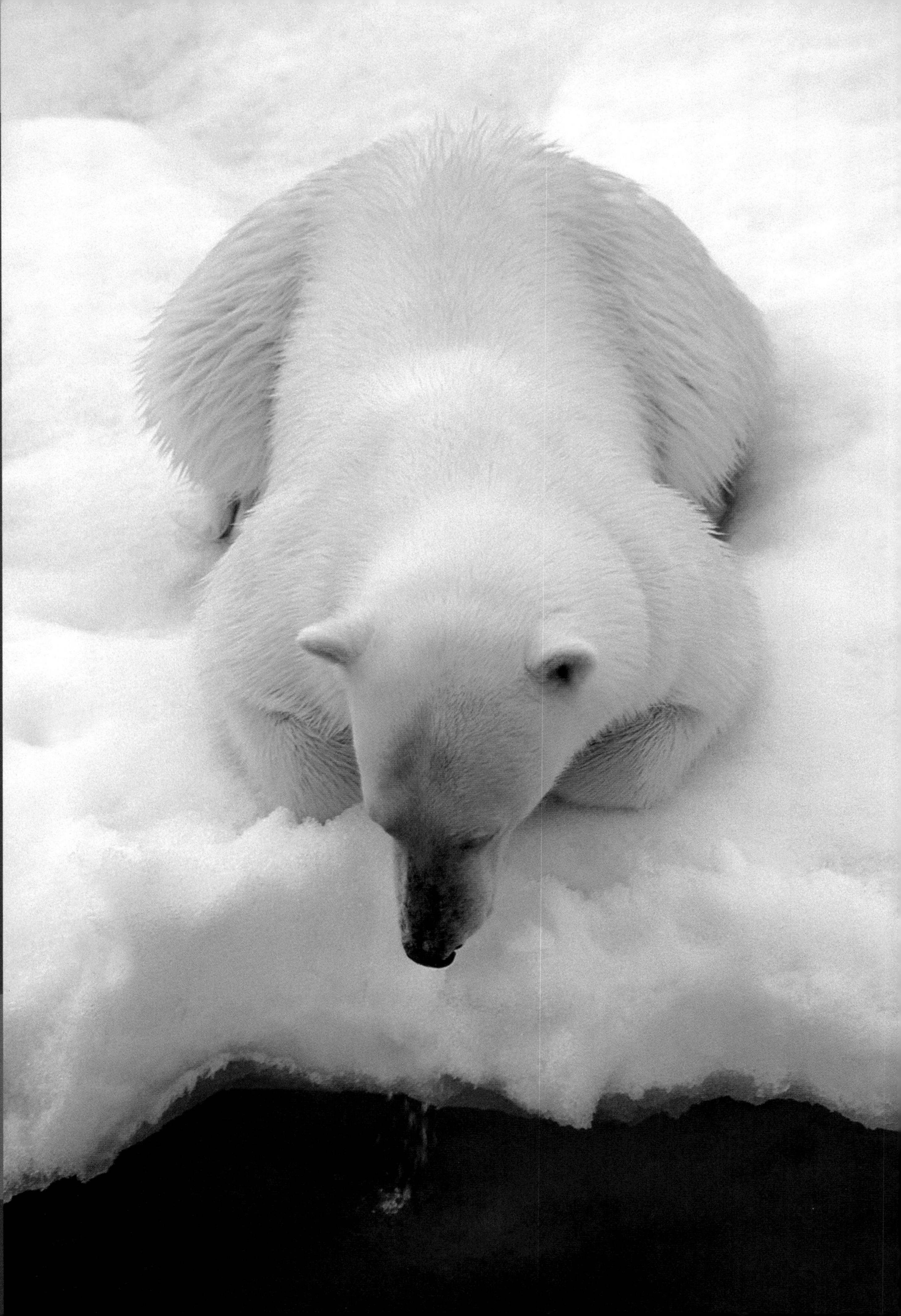

Polar bears spend a lot of time hunting, too. To catch a seal, polar bears sit by holes in the ice. They wait for seals to come to the holes for air. Then they grab the seals with their strong claws and teeth.

Polar bears stay very still when they are hunting

Today, some people go to see polar bears in the wild. Other people watch polar bears at zoos. Sometimes they can see the polar bears swimming underwater. It is exciting to see these big bears up close!

Polar bears are popular animals in many zoos

A *Polar Bear Story*

Why do bears have short tails? **Native Americans** used to tell a story about this. They said that a bear wanted to know how to fish in an icy lake. A fox told the bear to put his tail through a hole in the ice. The bear did. When he tried to pull his tail out, it was frozen in the ice and ripped off. From then on, bears had short tails!

Native Americans the first people to live in America before white people came

Read More

Canizares, Susan. *Polar Bears*. New York: Scholastic, 2002.

Miller, Debbie. *A Polar Bear Journey*. Boston: Little, Brown & Company, 1997.

Web Sites

Enchanted Learning: Polar Bears
*http://www.enchantedlearning.com/subjects/mammals/bear/
Polarbearcoloring.shtml*
This site has polar bear facts and a coloring page.

WWF Polar Bear Tracker
*http://www.panda.org/about_wwf/where_we_work/europe/what_we_do/
arctic/polar_bear/kids_zone/index.cfm*
This site has polar bear games and facts.